Sociopaths and Psychopaths:

Our True Intentions Revealed

I0407536

By: Ted Dawson

Table of Contents

Introduction

It is statistically likely that you have encountered a psychopath or sociopath in your lifetime. You have probably fallen victim to a psychopath or sociopath's cruel, manipulative games. You have been wounded by this sick, twisted person's refusal to acknowledge that you are a human being with feelings and needs. At least one percent of the human population is psychopathic, and psychopaths are three times more likely to be male than female. Twenty-five percent of male prisoners are believed to have antisocial and psychopathic tendencies. One percent of the population is comprised of sociopaths, as well.

You may meet a psychopath or sociopath anywhere - in the workplace, at school, in your family, or even your social spheres. If you have had the misfortune of being close to one of these people, then you undoubtedly understand how they are emotionally chiseled, uncaring, manipulative, and completely without empathy or sympathy. You also know just how much it can hurt trying to have a personal relationship with someone who falls into one of these categories.

I have encountered a few sociopaths and psychopaths in my time. For a while, I dated a sociopath. I also had a psychopathic roommate who robbed me blind. In addition, I have studied case studies about these people, including notable serial killers like Ted Bundy. I have learned the hard way how to protect myself against these terrible people. Now I want to share what I have learned with you.

First, this book will show you the signs of sociopaths and psychopaths so that you can spot these harmful people in your life and avoid them. Next, I will present some anecdotes from sociopaths and psychopaths that I have met and spoken with or that I have discovered detailed case studies about. From these anecdotes, you can gain a better understanding of how these people think and what their motives are. If these stories do not inspire you to run far away from these types of people, then I don't know what will. Finally, I will go over useful tips for defending yourself against sociopaths and psychopaths that may enter your life, and how to heal from the abuse and harm that these people can cause you mentally, emotionally, and even physically.

By the end of this book, you will be able to detect and deflect harmful sociopaths and psychopaths. You will also know how to cope with one of these people in your life if you cannot reasonably get away from them. You will have the tools necessary to lead a happy, healthy life without scars, drama, and pain caused by sociopaths and psychopaths. Your life will be much better when you become immune to the harm that these people can cause you.

There is no reason to suffer just so that a sociopath or psychopath can get some sadistic pleasure or some little thing that he or she wants. As a human being, you have value and you have basic rights. You deserve to be happy and to live your life free of the harm that these types of people will deliberately inflict upon you. Therefore, you should begin reading this book now and take action to protect yourself and make your life happier. Start the process of understanding and denying sociopaths and psychopaths their power.

Chapter 1: The Differences between Sociopaths and Psychopaths

Sociopaths and psychopaths are not the same creatures. However, they share many of the same traits. That is why many people use the two terms interchangeably. If you were to incorrectly diagnose someone in your life as a psychopath or sociopath when he is in fact the other, for example, you would not be entirely wrong because both types of people share many similarities in their behavior. But you should understand that there are differences between these two types of people.

It is easy to confuse psychopaths and sociopaths. Both are people with mental disorders that profoundly affect their characters and their behavior. Both are charming and good at manipulating people. In addition, both are potentially dangerous because they lack empathy and do not mind hurting others. They ruthlessly go after what they want. Often they are calculating, and plan things out far in advance.

You usually cannot win against either of these people if you try to argue with them.

Both psychopathy and sociopathy are defined as Antisocial Personality Disorders in the Diagnostic Statistical Manual. They share the following traits:

- A tendency to break the law
- A disregard for the rights of other human beings
- A complete lack of remorse or guilt for their actions
- A tendency toward violent behavior

However, this is where the similarities end. Sociopaths and psychopaths have many notable differences in their behavior. Understanding what you are dealing with is important so that you can gauge how to react to a sociopath or psychopath that you encounter in your life. In the following sections, I describe what these people are like. I use the term "he" for ease but sociopaths and psychopaths can also be female.

What Sociopaths are Like

Sociopaths are made by their environment while psychopaths are born that way. A sociopath generally learned his traits by being exposed to them. His environment shaped him into who he is today. Having a sociopathic family member increases his odds of being a sociopath, meaning that the mental disorder can be congenital. Some sociopaths have been found to possess lesioned regions within the brain, suggesting that their mental illness has a physical origin. Brain injuries or brain diseases can potentially cause sociopathy to develop.

Sociopaths are often prone to emotional outbursts. They are easily irritated, annoyed, and angered. Their emotions tend to get the best of them. Often, they are unstable people, who are unable to hold down jobs or remain in serious long-term relationships. It is possible for them to care about other people and even form emotional attachments to other human beings, but these attachments are typically created for their own benefit and do not last very long.

A sociopath is not above violence. However, his game is usually mental. He would prefer to hurt you mentally and play games with you, rather than physically harming you. Overall, he can be described as deceitful, calculating, and untrustworthy, underneath the beautiful façade that he erects for the world to see. He is manipulative and gets what he wants through various tactics. When you try to confront him, he will make you look crazy to the rest of the world while preserving his own appearance of innocence.

If a sociopath commits a crime, it will usually be because his emotions got the best of him. His crime will be haphazard and sloppy, committed in a fit of rage. A sociopath is usually not able to dissociate himself from his actions the way psychopaths can. However, he does share the ability of psychopaths to view other people as objects, rather than living beings with feelings and needs.

What a Psychopath is Like

Psychopaths are the products of Nature. A mixture of genetics and chemical imbalances in the brain create psychopathy. The brain of a psychopath is often smaller than that of a normal person with no diagnosed mental disorder. In addition, the brain of a psychopath often has signs of damage, such as legions, which are present from birth. Birth injuries or genetic problems are the most likely causes of this brain damage.

A psychopath is very conniving, like a sociopath. But his intent is to hurt you for the sheer thrill of gaining control over you. He has a predatory instinct and likes to prey on people. This is why he is more likely to plot a cold-blooded murder than a sociopath. Serial killers are prime examples of who psychopaths are: They kill just for the sheer enjoyment of it and they like to control people through horror, torture, and brutal violence.

A psychopath typically has no empathy. He may get his kicks from harming small animals or watching people fall. He may play cruel pranks and find them hilarious. His penchant for violence will be high. Though he may be good at pretending to be sorry or afraid, you will find after a while that these emotions are fake and that he really experiences no remorse. In addition, recent studies have connected psychopaths with a preference for bitter food. Psychopaths are more likely to drink their coffee black than other groups with different mental disorders.

In addition, a psychopath is very cool and collected. His emotions will never get the best of him, unlike a sociopath. If he commits a crime, it will be the perfect crime, executed with precision. Everything he does is planned out carefully and intricately. In this way, psychopaths tend to resemble reptiles because of their total emotional detachment from the things that they do.

What It Is like being with a Sociopath or Psychopath

Again, I use "he" simply for convenience in the following section.

Having a relationship with either a sociopath or a psychopath is a very bad idea. Both of these types of people are incredibly toxic. They are not made for relationships with other human beings. You will usually end up being a victim of controlling behavior, manipulation, and even deliberately malicious mind games and mental or even physical torture if you are involved with one of these people. Your partner will never respect your needs or take care of you emotionally; he is simply not equipped to. He also will never be sorry for anything that he does, and he will do whatever he wants, even if he knows that it will hurt you. Your feelings and needs simply will not matter. He will be adept at manipulating you so that you question your own sanity and feel like the guilty one, when in fact, you are the victim. He may bend your mind so that you believe that you are a terrible person and that you deserve the terrible things he does to you. Control is his ultimate aim. If you get out of a relationship with one of these people, you will suffer from low self-esteem and serious mental and emotional wounds. You will never quite be the same.

In order to better understand how psychopaths and sociopaths work, read Chapters 3 and 4. In these chapters, I use anecdotes from psychopaths and sociopaths to help you gain a thorough understanding of how their minds work.

Chapter 2: How to Spot Psychopaths and Sociopaths

It can be hard to know when a person is a sociopath or psychopath since these people tend to be great at putting on a charming social façade. But knowing the symptoms that sociopaths and psychopaths experience can help you identify them and put your guard up around them.

Inappropriate Emotional Reactions

Sociopaths and psychopaths are not normal when it comes to emotions. Therefore, these people will not know how to react in emotional situations. You may just be met with an inappropriate emotional reaction to a situation. A psychopath or sociopath will be angry most of the time. When not angry, they may laugh at a funeral or cry at a happy ending in a movie. Their emotions do not fit the situation. Sometimes, you may wonder if they even feel at all, or if they are just acting and pretending to have emotions.

Fake Emotions

Psychopaths and sociopaths are often good at faking emotions. But you will notice that their emotions are superficial. They may frown or cry or otherwise show an emotion, but their body language will not match what they are expressing. Somehow, they will slip up, giving away that they do not feel what they are saying that they feel.

Also, you should trust your gut. If you feel that someone is faking an emotion, then you are probably right. Someone who often fakes emotions is exhibiting a troubling sign of sociopathy or psychopathy.

Being Very Charming and Ingratiating

A sociopath or psychopath will be the most charming person that you ever meet. He will try his best to make you fall in love with him, literally or metaphorically. He will ramp up the charm so that he makes the ultimate best first impression.

A psychopath will ingratiate himself to you and put you in his debt. You think that he is being helpful, but really he is just calculating ways that he can gain your favor and your gratitude so that he can manipulate you more. Be wary of people who are willing to do exorbitantly huge favors for you, especially immoral or hurtful things to other people.

For instance, Jacob Wells, a diagnosed psychopath, stated that he will go to great lengths to get new acquaintances to like him. For example, if someone he is getting to know mentions that she hates a certain person in the office, he will offer to "get rid of" that person by somehow getting that person fired or otherwise out of the picture.

Certain Careers

Certain careers contain the most psychopaths and sociopaths. The skills and personality traits that these careers call for encourages the large number of Antisocial Personality Disorder sufferers to enter them

Lawyers, CEOs, and clergy members are some of the most likely to be psychopaths, studies have found. The lack of emotions, the cold-blooded drive to get things done no matter what the means and the manipulation required by these leadership positions make them ideal for psychopaths. Nonviolent psychopaths may excel in more scientific disciplines that call for a lack of emotion, as well.

Sociopaths are often drawn to careers that give them power and dominance as well. The careers that have the largest number of sociopathic members include CEOs, attorneys, salespersons, surgeons, doctors, journalists, policemen, and clergy members.

Speech Patterns

In a study of 52 convicted killers, researchers found that fourteen were psychopaths. They then interviewed these psychopathic killers about their crimes. They noticed that the psychopathic killers spoke about their crimes differently than non-psychopathic killers. The psychopathic killers consistently spoke in terms of cause-and-effect, showed no remorse or compassion for their victims, and focused on basic human needs like food or money. Emotions did not factor much into their speech. They seemed to view their crimes as the only logical step that they could take in some sort of plan that they had.

From this study, many researchers have reached the conclusion that psychopaths are needs-driven and goal-oriented. They are also relatively emotionless and don't like to speak about their emotions. Since most people will slip references to their own emotions into their speech naturally, you should watch out for people who don't. This is often a troubling sign that someone suffers from psychopathy.

Sociopaths also are relatively emotionless. In their speech, they will talk about themselves a lot. They will express anger or irritation, but few other emotions. Often, they do not talk about other people in a "we-oriented" way. Rather, they speak mostly using "I" terms and they only speak about other people in order to criticize them. Their needs rank before the needs of others, so they sound very selfish when they talk.

Pathological Lying

Sociopaths are pathological liars. If you repeatedly catch someone fabricating reality and telling lies, then you should beware. No normal person engages in that much lying.

Psychopaths can be liars as well, but their deception is usually part of their chameleon act. They will lie about who they are, for instance, to get you to like them. If you meet someone who does not appear to be who he says he is, then watch out. You may be dealing with a calculating and untrustworthy psychopath or a sociopath who can't control his impulse to lie.

Impulsivity

Sometimes, it is a good thing when people are spontaneous. These people often seem like more fun. But a more dangerous reality may underlie their impulsivity. People who act on impulses and do not think before they act are often dangerous. They can make huge mistakes and cause others harm. However, they also do not care about the consequences of their actions.

The next time you meet someone who is incredibly impulsive, be cautious. Observe him for other signs. If he has an unstable life because of his impulsivity and is known for rash and unwise decisions, he is probably a sociopath. Whether he is a sociopath or not, however, he is probably not the best person to hang out with anyway.

Law-Breaking

A psychopath or sociopath experiences no fear of the law. He will do what he wants, and he may even laugh at his willingness to break the law. Police and laws will seem funny to him. He will do whatever he wants without regard to these things. He acts without fear and seems to enjoy flouting the law.

Watch out for people who get a thrill from breaking the law or find it funny to commit crimes. This is actually not normal or admirable behavior. Anyone who is willing to flout the law so freely, probably has little remorse and little interest in respecting other rules, such as, rules you set for your personal boundaries.

Being Intensely Interesting

Most people report that they find psychopaths mesmerizing and intriguing, but they cannot honestly say why. The answer is that psychopaths are different from normal people. This makes them rather scary and fascinating. In addition, many psychopaths are good at making themselves seem like the most interesting people around.

A psychopath is an expert at reading people. Therefore, when he meets you, he will be able to tell right away what your likes and dislikes are in other people. He will pretend to possess these traits and look like a model person to you. He will fake certain interests and express certain opinions that make you feel drawn to him.

In addition, he will paint himself as a fabulous person with a flawless history. He will be the class genius or the class clown. He will be the charming, understanding, and the intoxicatingly smart date with the engaging dating profile and the knack for a deep conversation about whatever you want to talk about. In short, he will create an image of himself that is superficial but very interesting.

Sociopaths can also be interesting because they are charming and because they possess boundless confidence and self-esteem. They may be great at creating alluring first impressions. However, they usually are not as talented at keeping up the mirage as psychopaths. Relatively quickly, you will begin to notice holes in their images or discrepancies in their stories. You will realize that they are incredibly selfish and toxic people.

Inflated Ego

Both psychopaths and sociopaths have intact images of themselves. No matter how terrible they are or how poorly they are performing at life in general, they love themselves. They view themselves as superior and perfect.

If you meet someone who believes that he can do no wrong and is utterly perfect despite his glaring flaws, you may be dealing with a sociopath or psychopath. Watch out for people who have hyper-inflated egos. These people think that they are perfect and that you don't matter as much as they do.

Spotty History

Sociopaths especially are volatile and unreliable people. They tend to have spotty work and romantic histories. There will probably be gaps in their life stories that simply cannot be filled. They may have moved around a lot and they may have lived with family on numerous occasions, only to get thrown out time and time again.

When a sociopath shares his story, it will not make much logical sense. It will have holes and inexplicable gaps in it. It will also have a lot of tumult and upheaval. A sociopath's story will almost never be complete or wholesome.

Meanwhile, a psychopath's past may be perfect. But a psychopath will usually adapt himself to look perfect to you. He will lie about his past if necessary to make himself perfect. You may never find out the truth, but you will always wonder about this person's history. Certain things may not make sense since a psychopath will fabricate details. A psychopath may also be very discreet and may not share much information about himself, despite being obsessed with himself.

Manipulation

Manipulation is a huge sign that someone is a sociopath or psychopath. You do not want to spend time around manipulators period. Manipulation is a troublesome trait in people and a sign of toxicity. You want to avoid it at all costs.

Sociopaths are especially known for their conniving ways. Life is a game to them, and you are just another pawn for them to play. When you are in the presence of a sociopath, you will often find that you are being goaded to do things that you are not comfortable with. You may find it hard and even frightening to say no to sociopaths.

You may also find that a true sociopath is great at making you feel crazy. Psychopaths are also quite adept at this form of manipulation. Using guilt, threats, and fear tactics, these people will make you feel like you deserve what you are getting. They will make you feel so bad that you do what they want. If you confront them, they will make it seem like you are just being crazy or paranoid, they are masters of redirection, these people will make sure that you never win a confrontation or argument without looking and feeling bad.

A close personal relationship with one of these people will warp and twist your mind in horrible ways. You will feel less than human. You will believe that you deserve everything that you get in this toxic relationship and you will start to change yourself to please your manipulator.

When you get upset, your manipulator will never say sorry. Instead, he will make a game of making you feel as if you are somehow at fault.

A sociopath or psychopath will also never respect your boundaries as a person. When you set boundaries, he will manipulate you to get you to drop them. This person will never give up until he gets his way. Your rights and your needs simply do not matter. You will be amazed at how blatantly selfish he is.

Sooner or later, you will find that the sociopath or psychopath no longer has any use for you, and has moved on without a backward glance. After you have given everything that you possibly could to a sociopath or psychopath, you will find that you are still not appreciated.

Lack of Remorse

You will never hear a psychopath or sociopath say sorry, or if you do, he won't mean it. An utter lack of remorse is a troubling sign in any person and it may indicate underlying sociopathy or psychopathy. A sociopath or psychopath will always be able to justify each and everything he does, no matter how despicable it is.

He also won't hesitate to do bad things to other people. It is all OK in his head. He believes that the ends always justify the means. Especially in the case of psychopaths, everything he does is planned out ahead of time. His actions are part of a greater picture that you are not privy to. If you question his actions, even his most objectionable ones, he will not be sorry because he sees a greater picture that justifies everything that he does.

Cruel Sense of Humor

A psychopath may exhibit a very cruel sense of humor that relates to his need to control and hurt other people for his own sick emotional gratification. Psychopaths are the types of people who laugh hysterically when people fall and get hurt. They may find pranks such as "I just got a call and your mother died" are absolutely hilarious. The fact that they are laughing at the expense of others does not bother them since they enjoy pain and do not feel remorse or compassion of any kind.

Sociopaths also have no remorse and enjoy hurting others. Pain and suffering may be humorous to them as well. A sociopath is likely to use jokes and humor as a veiled weapon with which he insults and hurts you. Then, when you claim that you are hurt, he will simply say, "It was a joke! Get a sense of humor."

Denial of Your Rights as a Human Being

You will find that when you are in the presence of a sociopath or psychopath, your rights will not matter at all. This person will not mind hurting you. He will not respect your boundaries. When you say no, he will refuse to listen. He will not give you your autonomy or follow any rules that you make.

Remember that psychopaths and sociopaths do not view you as a person with feelings. Rather, you are a mere object to these people. In addition, these people do not mind flouting rules and breaking the law. Therefore, why would they care about manners, proper human etiquette, or the rules and boundaries that you set?

Chapter 3: From the Mind of a Sociopath

The following chapter is dedicated to anecdotes from the minds of various sociopaths. Some of these people are authors, while others are people that I have known and spoken with personally. Read this chapter to gain a sense of what life looks like in the mind of a sociopath.

M.E. Thomas

M.E. Thomas is a sociopath who authored the book *Confessions of a Sociopath: A Life Spent Hiding in Plain Sight*. In this book, she vividly describes her experiences as a sociopath getting by in normal society. One of her most memorable quotes is: "We are your neighbors, your co-workers, and quite possibly the people closest to you...." With this quote, she describes how common sociopaths are, and how easily they can blend into the mesh of society without being spotted. As a result, they are able to infiltrate the lives of their victims, because they do not appear to be monsters. The most normal-looking guy could be a sociopath underneath his unassuming guise.

M.E. Thomas is not a violent person. Nevertheless, she often has thrilling fantasies about killing her father and other people, such as a Metro employee who disrespected her. Hurting animals also appeals to her, as she killed a baby possum that she could have rescued from a pool. She loves thrills, and she loves adrenalin rushes. She also loves flouting social norms and conventions. Her talent for deceit is unsurpassed; she is able to lie convincingly and fool everyone in her life. While she knows that she is a sociopath, she has high self-esteem and believes that she is a great person. She also has never experienced empathy and cannot pick up on the feelings or needs of other people, not that she cares about that too much. People in her life are objects that she likes to toy with to get a reaction. Sometimes she even conducts experiments on the people around her, just for thrills. She believes that her heart is "colder and blacker" than the hearts of most people, which is why she believes she enjoys breaking others' hearts so much. Her entire book is written from a self-absorbed, narcissistic point of view, which is certainly characteristic of a sociopath.

She admitted in her book that often she cannot feel like other people can. In college, she writes that she had a friend who experienced an intense loss. Instead of feeling bad for her friend, Thomas just became frustrated that her friend was no longer fun. Thomas often finds that she must fake emotions that she doesn't really feel. She didn't even cry when her father used to beat her with a belt.

Overall, she leads a normal life, just like the other four percent of the population that shares her diagnosis. She estimates that at least one in twenty-five people are sociopaths, so you probably have met someone like her, living a normal life and hiding a terrible diagnosis behind a normal mask. As an attorney, she is successful and able to take care of herself. She views her sociopathy as a great trait that allows her to excel in her life.

Thomas's sociopathy is a likely product of her childhood. She had a violent, abusive father and an emotionally masochistic and hysterical mother. Her mother did not offer her much emotional support or protection from her father, and in fact was usually indifferent to her suffering. This upbringing hardened M.E. Thomas and led to her turning off her emotionality. In addition, she writes that she has a genetic predisposition to this condition.

Every few years, Thomas suffers from what she calls "destructions" of her life. This is when she loses a job, friend, or boyfriend because of her deception and manipulation. Things backfire on her, causing her strife and instability in her life. She must struggle to live normally. As of the time of her writing, she suffered difficulty finding a new job. This instability is typical of sociopaths.

Joseph Carlos

The following is a personal anecdote from a person that I know who is a sociopath. I will refer to him as Joseph, even though that is not his real name. While this piece is fictional, it is based entirely on direct quotes that Jose has told me over the years that I have known him. Here is his story:

I am a meth user and I still live in my parents' house. I am living here until I get married; it's the Mexican way. My family is from Mexico and I am a proud Mexican American. I have had many girlfriends, most of whom eventually just left because they couldn't handle what I tried to show them. I have loved each of these women and I insist on staying in contact with them because our bonds shouldn't end just because we break up. Only one of my exes refuses to talk to me; all the others can't get enough of me. I don't understand why people are so drawn to me, yet they can't handle me.

I am more intelligent than most of the population. At one point, I even broke the Internet. I cannot describe how, but it was amazing. I find patterns in things that other people just can't see. No one sees the world the way that I do. I feel like I have been blessed with a unique sight. Sometimes I will sit in my room and talk with God for days. He's a funny man and he has a lot to say. He has chosen me to be his Apostle, but I am just waiting for my time to spread the word. I don't think most people are able to hear the word yet.

My best friend in the world thought I was annoying when we first met at an old job. He kept telling me to shut up. I do talk a lot. Now he loves me. I go over there to watch football and drink sometimes. Usually, I'm too busy, though. I have another friend who comes to see me sometimes. He is a drug dealer. For a while, I lived with him in a drug den and I didn't bathe for three months. That's my record and I'm so proud of it. It was hilarious how people would wrinkle their noses up at me and grimace when I came around.

People always try to change me. It is my job to show them that I have unlocked the secret to the universe. I am an enlightened person and I believe that others should see things the way that I do. It would end the suffering in the world. Most people resist my attempts to bring them to the light, so I just work on them until they give in. I have been able to bring a few people to the light.

I turned off my sexual desire years ago. Now, I enjoy withholding sex from my girlfriends. They get so frustrated. I hope to break them down and show them that sex is not the most important thing in the world. I also try to show my family that I don't have to do the things that they ask me to. Life is so much more important than the silly needs that people have. People would be so much happier if they stopped expecting their needs to be met and stopped making such high demands.

I know that I have succeeded in breaking someone when I make him or her cry for hours. It is my goal to do this. By unleashing so much pain on others, I bring them a little bit closer to enlightenment. Plus, it thrills me to watch other people cry. People are all so weak and they break so easily. I like to test people to see what they're made of. They are almost never as tough as they like to say they are. I believe that I am doing them a favor and that this is all for their greater good. They're learning valuable lessons from me. I train people on how to fence mentally. Recently I made my sister cry for hours because I refused to give her the money she lent me a few weeks ago. She just wanted to go get drunk and high, so I had a right to refuse to pay her back. I owe a lot of people money, but money is not important. People need to realize that. They need to put their material needs away and place more value in their friendships with me. If they can't do that, then they certainly don't deserve any money from me.

Meth is my best friend. It enables me to stay up for days, playing games on my phone. People think that I just waste my time. They don't see how I'm training for battle. The games help me grow stronger. Plus, I do not change on meth, even though everyone thinks that I do. Meth just makes me more of who I am. Some people have diagnosed me with sociopathy and narcissism, but I think that mental health is a myth. I am perfect the way that I am and people who judge me just don't understand enlightenment when they see it. There is a reason why I act the way that I do, and I will not change just to fit into the standards that society has set for people.

Most of my memories and stories go back to age seventeen. I do not remember much from my twenties. I grew up in LA and now I live in a small town in the Southwest desert. I get jobs because I am fluent in both Spanish and English and I am a rapid translator. My brain is just wired to handle languages exceptionally well.

One of the funniest things for me is to see girls play their games. They think that they can control me but I refuse to ever be broken down. I have the strongest will that anyone will ever come across. When girls start their crap, I just twist it back on them. People hate that. It's hilarious to watch how confused and upset girls get. My sister is one of my favorites to mess with. I also like messing with my girlfriends.

My sister feels entitled because she works so much. All she does is shovel Chinese fast food into Styrofoam boxes. I have had a lot of jobs, but I usually walk out. I don't know why, but nothing can hold me in chains. Most of my jobs just don't interest me. Once I worked in a fast food establishment; that was so boring that I quit. I also was a manager of a movie theater for a while and they fired me for having drugs. It's their loss. I was the best movie projectionist there and I was the cool manager that everyone liked.

Sick Boy

Whether or not you have read the book or seen the movie *'Trainspotting,'* there is a character within the book named Simon Murphy who was called Sick Boy by his friends. Sick Boy displays many of the signs of sociopathy. Characters like him in real life are harmful, toxic people who should be avoided in your best interests. Here is Sick Boy's profile:

Sick Boy is very charming. This is how he is able to pick up women whenever and wherever he wants. He loves flaunting the ease with which he gets laid to his friends. He appears sweet, friendly, and good-looking on the surface, but underneath his charming façade, he is just sizing people up to find out how he can scam them. Constantly, he runs scams and hurts people, just to get money to feed his heroin habit.

At one disturbing point in both the movie and the book, Sick Boy's baby asphyxiates to death. The mother is devastated and balms her pain by doing more heroin. Sick Boy seems initially upset, but soon he appears to get over his grief and become an even worse person than he was before. He throws himself into crime and heroin use with a vengeance.

In the end of the book and movie, he joins his friends in a huge heroin deal that makes them all wealthier than ever before. He casually mentions that he would make off with all of the money and steal his friends' shares if he had the chance. He says this with absolutely no trace of remorse or guilt; he simply is telling the truth about how easily and emotionlessly he is willing to hurt other people for his own benefit.

Throughout the book, Sick Boy is shown as someone with literally nothing real under the surface. He appears smart, capable, and charming, but in reality, he has no talents and no interests beyond hurting others for his own benefit. While he is calculating, he is far from a psychopath, since he is capable of emotion and often his plots are performed so sloppily that he does not get exactly what he wants. He has nothing to prove that he is better than his friends, so he attempts to convince them that he is better by showing off how easily he can pick up women. He also enjoys showing off how he is able to control his heroin addiction more easily than the other characters in the group of friends that he runs with. Competitiveness is one of the major traits of being a sociopath. Simply put, they will go to any extreme to prove that they are more capable than everyone else.

Darby Crash

Born Jon Paul Beahm, Darby Crash was the lead singer of the punk band '*The Germs.*' Darby Crash reached international acclaim after he committed a ritualistic suicide via intentional heroin overdose when he was only twenty-two years old. As a child, Darby Crash had a rough relationship with his mother, and his father was absent from his life. He lost one of his siblings to a heroin overdose and was exposed to drugs from an early age. From a young age, he was incredibly charming and charismatic, with lots of friends. He was expelled from an alternative school for "brainwashing" other students. Always a leader, he was able to attract people and get them to do what he wanted.

After being expelled, Darby Crash started *'The Germs.'* The band broke up in 1980 due to increasing violence at all of their shows. Shortly after, Darby Crash attempted to create a cult. The cult was supposed to end in a ritual mass suicide. However, only his girlfriend at the time joined him in suicide.

Like most sociopaths, Darby Crash was very charming. People felt drawn to him. However, there was no reason for people to like him. People had difficulty explaining just why they liked him so much. He had a violent temper, was very controlling, and had extremely odd ideas. He was more than willing to flout the conventions and laws of society, which was why he chose punk music as an avenue for the expression of his antisocial philosophy. Though he often had calculated plans, he usually did not execute them well, and his results were usually sloppy and undisciplined. Now he has attained international fame for his despicable actions.

Christine's Boyfriend

A girl whom I will call Christine wrote into a forum asking for help in dealing with her sociopathic boyfriend, whom I will call Fred. She was beside herself and didn't know how to handle breaking up with Fred. Though they had been together for two years, she had come to hate him.

Fred would never introduce Christine to his friends. He finally admitted that he didn't want her to see the type of person he was around his friends. His entire life was cloaked in secrecy and he would pathologically lie about everything possible. One time a girl called him and asked for him by name. When he answered the phone, the girl reminded him that they had a date. He hung up on her, told Christine that he didn't know the girl, and claimed that this was probably an elaborate plot to lure him somewhere and rob him.

His deception extended to his personality. He would show different masks to different people, pretending to adopt different personalities to please people. This was part of his charm, but it was also a bad sign about his mental wellness.

In addition, Fred thoroughly enjoyed hurting people. For instance, he stole some memorabilia from someone who had never done anything to him. The memorabilia was not valuable in any way, but Fred chose to keep it just to hurt the person whom he had stolen it from. During fights, he would become extremely nasty and volatile to Christine, and he was often irritated with her. He was great at hurting her.

When Fred exhibited emotion, it was usually fake. He would fake cry, with no water coming out from his tear ducts. The only real emotion he seemed to feel was anger. He was often angry and he would take it out on Christine.

Perhaps the creepiest experience that Christine ever had with Fred involved her little dog. When Fred first met the dog, he seemed to be nice to it. However, after a while, the dog acted afraid of Fred and would hold its tail between its legs and yelp at him. Christine witnessed Fred chasing the dog with a tennis racket once. Hurting this animal seemed to give Fred immense joy. Christine said a scary and depraved light would shine in his eyes as he tortured the innocent dog.

Christine was scared to break up with Fred. She worried that he might somehow hurt her. She did not feel that he was above killing her dog. Getting away from this man was of paramount importance to her, but she was not sure how. Her fear arose from the sociopath's uncanny ability to manipulate and hurt others.

Tim

Tim is the fictional name that I gave a boy who was receiving treatment for drug addiction, bipolar disorder, and antisocial disorder. We got together for a few talks and he shared the following revelations about his life with me:

I have a lot of friends. Recently, my friends decided to stop talking to me, so I'm busy finding new friends. All this drama started because I got into a fight while I was drunk. People are always telling me that I can't handle my liquor, but nobody is the boss of me. I like to drink and I don't think I drink too much. The real reason that I got into a fight was because this guy was being a jerk and he attacked me first, claiming that I was hitting on his girlfriend. I was because she was hot. He didn't need to attack me for that.

Anyway, this guy attacked me. Now I got mad and I attacked him back. I ended up pulling out a knife that I carry around with me. I just couldn't lose the fight and lose face in front of my friends. The guy lost his nose, and I laughed when I saw that I had cut the tip off. Now my friends won't talk to me and I'm facing assault charges, just for defending myself. Plus, my job fired me because I couldn't show up for my shift the next day because I was in jail. Like, sorry I couldn't come in for your stupid job because I was held against my will in a jail cell.

I find that the world is very irritating and unfair. Sometimes I fantasize about throttling people or cutting off more than just the tips of their noses. I know this isn't normal, but these fantasies make me feel a little bit better. People deserve to suffer for how they try to hurt me.

Recently my girlfriend cheated on me. She broke up with me. I went over to her house and convinced her that I love her and that it was wrong of her to leave me. I knew that I was winning when she smiled at me a certain way. Now we're back together and I'm plotting how to dump her and really break her heart. I think I'll let her catch me in bed with someone. She needs to pay. I only started dating her again just so that I could hurt her the way that she hurt me.

My family is pretty broken up. I haven't heard from my mom in years. For all I know, she's dead. I guess that's sad. My whole family is pretty sad. But I have never cried over them. They chose that path and I chose mine. I've been on my own since I was sixteen. I'm tough like that. I don't really care what my family does. I didn't pick them, so I don't have to deal with them. Sometimes I hit up my sister for help with money and sometimes she does help me. I make her feel bad for how she used to hit me and how she's my sister but she doesn't call me, so she shells out a few bills for me. One time she wouldn't help me even though I was homeless, so I made her boyfriend break up with her by telling him how she cheats on him every night with a different guy. That was so funny. She won't speak to me now, but I know that I can eventually wear her down when I need her again.

Right now I'm sleeping on my friend Mikey's couch, but he doesn't want me around anymore. He says that I have to find somewhere by the end of the week. So my living situation is up in the air, but I'm not too worried. Mikey has some expensive video game stuff that I can steal and pawn so that I can afford to stay in a motel until I meet someone new who will let me crash on their couch. Maybe I'll meet a new girlfriend who will let me move in. I meet people very easily and I always make friends easily. I'm just a really fun guy, the life of the party. I always know exactly what people want and how to give it to them, so people love me. Chicks especially dig me. I can have a different girl every night if I want.

At one point, I was a manager at an Arby's and I had my own place. I used to throw amazing parties there. But I lost it all after they found out that I was stealing food from work for my parties. Well, people love free food, so I had to steal it just to make everyone happy. I could tell that my boss was angry with me when I came into work one day because of how he was staring at me. I tried to pin it off on this other worker, but they had me on camera. I then tried to say that I was starving and that I needed the food but they didn't care. Fast food is so inhuman. They couldn't bother to see how badly I was suffering and how good I was at my job. They'd rather lose their best manager than sustain some losses of food inventory. Not like their food is that pricey, anyway. We're not talking about gourmet here.

I was mad, so after that, I found a homeless guy and beat the crap out of him. It was actually pretty funny. He was so scared that he finally ran away, abandoning his shopping cart full of useless crap. I went through the shopping cart but there wasn't anything that I wanted in there so I just pushed it off into a drainage ditch. Let him come back and pick it all up, covered in mud.

I guess that I enjoy hurting people. When people ask me, "Don't you feel bad about what you did?" I don't know how to answer. Of course I don't feel bad. Does anyone truly feel bad? I think we all get a little sick enjoyment out of being cruel.

Well, I'm very smart. One of these days I'm going to become a neuroscientist. Just watch. No one believes in me, but they don't know what they're dealing with. I'm actually quite smart and quite strong. I can do it. I just need to find a rich girlfriend who will pay my way. I'll even settle for a boyfriend, a sugar daddy if I have to. I know someone who got with a sugar daddy and his sugar daddy bought him two cars. Since I don't have a car, that would work out really perfect for me.

Jolene

Jolene was a landlady that I rented a room from. While she was always respectful toward me, she exhibited a great deal of alarming and controlling behavior toward others in her life:

My friend Cliff and I have known each other since high school. It is adorable how in love with me he is. I would never date him, but it's cute to watch him fawn over me. He is renting a room from me and I like to walk by his room wearing just a towel. He practically drools. I have fifteen other guys who all trip over me. Men can't get enough of me so I keep them around to use them for different things. They're always handy for repairs around the casita I own.

I'm one of the best decorators around. Sometimes I spend too much money on decorations. I don't care because my house looks stunning. If I ever need money, I usually just tell some guy that I need an abortion. You'd be shocked at how fast guys pay up when they think that you are carrying their kid.

My tenant has a dog that I hate. It yips all night. The other night I couldn't take it anymore so I let the dog out onto the street and chased it beating it with a broom until it ran away. It was hilarious hearing the dog yelp in pain and fear. Now, my tenant is crying and put signs up all over the neighborhood. I pretended to help her look for the dog, but I know that dog probably just got hit by a car. He isn't coming back, that's for sure. It's so hilarious how she doesn't even suspect that I drove the dog away. At least he won't be bothering me anymore while I try to sleep.

I have tons of friends. Everyone likes me. I really can't stand to be alone. When I'm alone, I feel like I'm going crazy. One of my tenants complained that I party too much so I evicted her. She claimed that she didn't have anywhere to go and I didn't let her back in until she got on her knees and apologized to me. It was hilarious. Other girls just envy me. But I'm like a goddess. My family doesn't talk to me, but they all suck. I don't miss them at all. My dad is an alcoholic and that's probably why I drink so much gin. I love gin. I love getting drunk, obnoxious and getting kicked out of bars.

Chapter 4: From the Mind of a Psychopath

The following stories are real-life anecdotes from actual diagnosed psychopaths. Some of these have been taken from people who write about their psychopathic disorders and struggles on the website Quora; others are based on interviews with people that I have met personally. I have changed all names so that these people cannot be personally identified.

Shayna (who Writes for Quora)

People assume that psychopaths are serial killers and terrible people. I don't think I'm either of those things. I am just an ordinary girl who views the world in a different way than most. I wouldn't even say that I'm sick, even though people like to think of psychopathy as a mental disorder.

I see nothing wrong with what I do or who I am. I just observe more keenly than most. I know that I need certain masks to survive; that is called facial mimicry by psychologists, but to me, it's just being a normal human being, fitting in, not acting like a freak. Sure, I lie and manipulate, but if you study other people, everybody engages in some form of deception and manipulation. It is required for survival. It does not make me a cold-blooded criminal.

Since I was young, I sensed that I was different. I always thought that I was just a solid, non-emotional, and keenly observant person. Only when I was nineteen was I diagnosed as a psychopath. The diagnosis made me laugh at first. Then I read up on psychopaths and realized that perhaps I am one. But being a psychopath hardly makes any difference to me. I do not allow that label to make me feel like a terrible person. I'm just another human being who happens to be a little different, thanks to my brain structure and high IQ.

Shiloh (who Writes for Quora)

I grew up using my little sister as a scapegoat. When I did something bad and I knew that I was going to be in trouble, I would blame her. I was an expert at twisting the truth so that she really did always look guilty. Then, when she would cry, I would get a certain thrill. Now I am sorry. I know that I shouldn't have done that. You are not supposed to hurt other human beings. I have learned this over time. It was a lesson, not a part of my natural instinct. I have to fight the urge to hurt people sometimes because I have learned that I am not supposed to do that.

I guess you could say that I don't have feelings. But I do have respect. I care about my family. Should something happen to them, I would not like that. My parents have worked hard and done many things for me over the years, so they have earned my respect. I also respect my sister, since she has withstood much abuse by me over the years and still turned into a model citizen and straight-A student.

The rest of my family is of little consequence to me. They did not raise me and they do not help me financially, so I see no point in keeping in contact with them. My Christmas card list is short.

Psychopathy requires discipline and control. Every day I must remember how I am supposed to act. Often it is not the same as how I want to act. I have to remember to smile, laugh, cry, grimace in disgust; I have to display these emotions, even if I don't feel them inside. I also have to pay attention to social settings so that I know exactly when to turn on the correct emotional response. Over the years, I have learned to fake empathy and to show people respect, even if they have done nothing to earn it.

Overall, most people would never guess that I am a psychopath. I'm sure they would run away in terror if they knew. In fact, a lot of people seem drawn to me. I don't mind that since connections are always useful. The more friends I have, the better. I am always looking forward to meeting new people. Most people don't know that I am a psychopath because I am good at pretending to care. That is because people like that and respond well to it. Over the years, I have learned how to act normal, so that I have it down to algorithms in my head. For example, I know that I should act sad when a friend is crying over a break-up or when someone dies.

However, I'm not a big party animal. Being social is a bit tiring when you are basically just putting on a huge charade. I do well in school and I focus on my grades. That is my main priority right now. I don't date because love is for procreation and I know that I would be a terrible parent. So what is the point of dating?

Life is simple. I am good at anything that I do. That is because I am careful to give everything my best effort and to always plan ahead. I am actually glad to be a psychopath because it allows me to dedicate my time and energy to useful pursuits, like going to school.

James Fallon

James Fallon is a neuroscientist who discovered his own psychopathy in 2005. His brain structure matched that of many famous serial killers whom he was studying. Though he had trouble believing that he was a psychopath, his friends and family were not surprised. Fallon decided to use his discovery to unlock answers about how psychopaths think and behave.

At first, he assumed that he could beat his psychopathy. But he could not. He realized that he did not have violent tendencies because of how well he was raised. Doctors were amazed that he had not committed suicide as a teenager because of the sheer level of damage in his brain. However, he does admit to having many psychopathic traits, such as a total lack of empathy, lack of feeling, and inability to connect to others on an emotional level. Most people know him as loud, funny, and charming, though his close friends who have known him for two years or longer all agree that he is undoubtedly a psychopath.

It is quite possible for psychopaths to lead normal lives. Fallon is a post-doc graduate and a successful neuroscientist. He is nonviolent and has a social life and a loving family.

Dave

Dave was a diagnosed psychopath that I actually lived with him for a short while. During his time living on my couch, he exhibited many behaviors that caused me to diagnose him as a psychopath. After a few months there, he actually received a formal diagnosis from a psychiatrist at a mental hospital that he was sent to. He was officially an Antisocial Personality Disorder with psychopathic tendencies.

My experiences with Dave were a bit stressful and scary at times. Dave came to live with me after his parents threw him out. He arrived with a car stuffed with a few clothes and two huge boombox speakers. He tried to sleep with me the first night, but I banished him to the couch. He did not seem too hurt by the rejection.

For the next few weeks, Dave lived on the couch. He spent most of his time abusing people on XBOX Live. Playing video games was very important to him and he always had to win or he would go into a conniption. He enjoyed tormenting people on XBOX Live, saying the rudest and most insulting and vulgar things that he could think of. Often, he would brag about mean things that he said online; he took pride in being an offensive "troll" and he found it hilarious when people got angry with him. One of the things that delighted him the most was when he would receive hate mail from people that he had angered online.

He didn't speak to his parents. When he spoke about them, it was without warmth. They were like an ATM to him and now that they would not support him, he didn't care about them anymore. Mostly he focused on his social life. He was an incredibly social person, with countless friends. He often went out to parties. He wanted a girlfriend and was extremely upset that women avoided him like the plague. He would do favors for girls, expecting that they would sleep with him in exchange. When that didn't happen, he would become angry and he would plot an elaborate revenge. Sometimes he would follow through on the revenge, as well.

The reason Dave left was because he robbed my house and took all the valuables to sell for a girl who was addicted to meth. Apparently, he used the money to buy her drugs. She actually did sleep with him, which appeared to make him very happy. He never spoke to me again. Despite all the kindness that my roommates and I had shown him, he had no qualms about robbing us blind when it suited his purpose of getting laid.

Chapter 5: How to Deal with a Sociopath or Psychopath in Your Life

With so many psychopaths and sociopaths present in the world population, it is quite possible that you have encountered at least one such person in your lifetime. You will actually probably encounter more than one Antisocial type. While scientists estimate that only one percent of the population is psychopathic and one percent is sociopathic, there is the possibility that even more of these people exist and simply have not been diagnosed.

Therefore, you need to be prepared for how to cope with such toxic presences in your life. You also need to know how to protect yourself against their wily ways. Never assume that you can defend yourself against one of these monsters because you probably will not be able to. Their charm, wit, and manipulation are usually so skillful that you will be caught unaware.

Protect Yourself against Antisocial Types

Don't Play

The easiest and best way to handle sociopaths and psychopaths is to not even waste your time dealing with them. The minute that you spot someone with the warning signs that I listed above or who seems like the people described in Chapters 3 and 4, you should immediately run the opposite way. Resist the charm that these people sport and protect yourself by putting distance. Refuse to accept favors from these people. Don't hang out with them or live with them. Do not go on a second date, or third, or whatever date you are on. Stop answering their calls and they will soon get bored and move on, even tho they are naturally persistent, do not give into their cons, you will need to develop the willpower and the persistence, even more than that of the Sociopath and Psychopath to ensure your own mental, emotional and physical safety.

It is very tempting to play the games that these antisocial personality types throw at you. These people are good at reading people, and they will design games and emotional hooks that will successfully bait you. But you must resist the urge to take this bait. You will not win. The best way to win is to simply not play. These types of people are very adept and practiced at their games, and winning is all they have to live for. You bet that they are going to win at your expense. Never expect for someone with one of these disorders to stop playing games or to let you win to preserve your feelings. Your feelings simply do not register as important to these people.

However, it is not always possible to do this. You may be dealing with a co-worker, family member, or another individual who has to be in your life. You may be so involved with this person that getting away carries a lot of risks and you are scared. Running away is simply not an option. If you are trapped in a desperate and unhealthy situation like this, then you will want to read on for more tips on how to protect yourself and get away from these horrible people.

Keep Power

Sociopaths and psychopaths are driven by a desire for power. Therefore, they try to control and get power over you in conversation. One of the best ways to guard yourself against a sociopath is to refuse to give him or her any power over you.

Do not make the assumption that sociopaths will back down out of love. They do not feel love. They will never submit to spare your feelings, even if they see that they are hurting you. Psychopaths actually thrive on human suffering and will only feel stronger if you show that you are in pain. Do not show that they are hurting you and do not expect them to stand down. Instead, keep your own power by wearing a stony mask of no emotion and refusing to reveal your pain or frustration.

Remember, this is all a game to the person that you are dealing with. You cannot hope to win by playing. Since you must interact with this person and cannot just walk away, you want to avoid playing his or her games the best that you can. The best way to do this is to keep your power to yourself.

How can you hold onto your own power? You can do this in two ways. The first way that you accomplish this is by refusing to give the person what he or she wants. He or she is probably after something – your anger, your resignation, your submission. Staunchly refuse to give it. Don't give an emotional reaction or do anything else that the person seems to be pushing for.

The second way is to maintain a calm, cool demeanor. Don't follow the person's arguments or buy into his or her games. Just smile, be pleasant, and be cool. Keep doing what you were doing. You can even ignore the person's attempts to get some sort of action or reaction from you.

By doing these two things, you hold onto your power. You also prevent yourself from getting hurt. Be very cautious around these people, however.

Don't Fall for Their Shenanigans

Someone who has the indicators of a sociopath or psychopath is probably not right in the head. Go with your gut and assume that this person is dangerous. So if this person does something kind-hearted or sweet, don't fall for it. Don't think, "Oh, but he sent me flowers when my mom died, so he can't be that bad of a guy." A sociopath or psychopath is perfectly capable of doing something kind in order to manipulate you into trusting him or her. There is always an ulterior motive behind the nice action. If such a person does something nice for you, say thank you, but either refuse the gesture or the gift, or accept it but do not let it sway your resolve and influence your reasoning. Don't try to rationalize what your gut tells you and convince yourself to trust this person.

These people are also quite charming. Do not let that charming façade fool you. In fact, if someone seems perfect or very alluring, you should put your guard up. Some people are just charming, but charm is typically superficial and a sign that someone is not who they say they are.

Finally, sociopaths and psychopaths are great at creating mirages to manipulate you. It is best to not believe anything that they tell you. If a person of this character starts telling you some story that causes your emotions to roil, stop and consider that they are probably just emotionally manipulating you. Definitely, don't believe what they say if they claim that they are trying to watch out for others or be good Samaritans. They are too self-serving to ever do good for anyone besides themselves.

Resist the Drama

Sociopaths and psychopaths are often adroit at causing serious drama among people. They do this in order to act out their own elaborate and hidden plans for ends that are probably completely unknown to you. Understand that drama will start between people in the presence of a sociopath or psychopath. It is best to stay out of this drama, or else you are just playing into the plot.

A good sign that an antisocial type of person is present is when a normally peaceful group of people suddenly dissolves into dramatic chaos. A peaceful, harmonious office will suddenly explode in fighting as everyone begins to perceive one another as enemies, thanks to clever rumors that the sociopath spreads. A marriage may sudden result in suspicions and fighting as a sociopath poisons both parties with toxic suggestions about the other partner. A couple may suddenly find themselves in a hateful and hurtful love triangle, with a sociopath in the center causing trouble. The sociopath's only goal is to create chaos in order to get others fired and earn a promotion, or to break up a marriage, or to steal away someone's romantic partner.

When drama starts to arise, just stay out of it. Don't partake in the gossip or believe the rumors. Don't confront people based on hearsay. Become very suspicious of the people who tell you hurtful things that other co-workers may have said or done behind your back; you should consider that these people may be stirring up trouble for some ulterior motive. By not buying into the drama, you avoid giving the sociopath what he or she wants and your life will be much more peaceful and healthy.

Keep Conversations Neutral

There will be times when you are forced to talk to a sociopath or psychopath. You will notice the signs that you learned about in this book. You will know that you need to have your guard up. But how do you carry on a normal conversation without getting yourself into hot water with this highly manipulative, cunning person?

It is possible that you may slip at some point. Don't beat yourself up over this. It is normal to feel charmed by one of these people and overshare. However, for the most part, you need to be guarded. Protect yourself and those you love by maintaining an incredibly neutral façade around toxic people of this nature.

You do not want to be too emotional in your interactions with this person. Keep a neutral little smile or serious expression on your face. Only discuss business. Don't even mention some normal tidbits about your life or who you are as a person, as even the tiniest tidbits can be deadly when shared with a sociopath or psychopath. Keep the conversation very focused on whatever business you two have at hand. If the sociopath or psychopath tries veering the conversation in other directions, just politely and firmly say, "I don't want to talk about that. Let's talk about this." In this way, you protect yourself and take charge of the conversation. You keep the ball in your court, rather than letting the sociopath or psychopath get a foothold and a little bit of control.

Never Divulge Confidential Details

Confidential information should always be kept to yourself. But this is particularly true when you are dealing with a harmful antisocial personality type. These people are very capable of crimes such as identity theft, or even using your information to frame you for their crimes. Make sure that you never share information such as your social security number, address, or other private details. Never let a sociopath or psychopath around your children, significant other, or pets, as these are very vulnerable things that the person may use to get to you and hurt you. In addition, never let this person into your home if you can help it. They may steal your most beloved belongings or otherwise use your home for their own nefarious purposes. Finally, make sure that important and sensitive documents, such as your license, never falls into the hands of such a person. You want to lock up your precious belongings and personal information around a Sociopath and a Psychopath.

Don't Lend a Sociopath or Psychopath Anything

Don't try to be a good friend and help one of these people out. These people can never feel gratitude and they will never appreciate what you do for them. Instead, they will mistake your kindness for weakness and take advantage of you. They also will throw you away and hurt you when they find out that you no longer serve them any useful purposes. Believe me, these people are cold-hearted and nothing you can do will protect you from the bite of their lack of conscience.

It is best not to invite these people into your life. So don't be a friend or a hero. Don't offer them your car, money, or a place to crash. The minute you start helping a sociopath or psychopath, you are opening yourself up to great harm. Just keep these types of people at arm's length and do not offer them assistance of any kind. When it's all said and done, whatever help you give to them, will be viewed as an obligation, and there is absolutely nothing you can do or say to convince them otherwise

The reverse is also true. If a sociopath or psychopath offers you help, be very cautious about accepting it. This person is not offering out of the goodness of his or her heart. He or she has no goodness in his or her heart. There is a guarantee that an ulterior motive exists. Most likely, this person is trying to put you in a position of debt and gratitude so that he or she can manipulate you and call on you for favors in the future. It is best to either refuse help or accept it with great caution and wariness. Be prepared to owe this person something in the future if you ever accept his or her help in any way.

Don't Share Vulnerable Details

Never admit to a sociopath what makes you happy or what makes you mad. If you do this, then you hand this person the key to your emotional states. Now he or she knows how to manipulate you and pull your emotions around like a marionette.

The things that hurt you, frighten you and give you joy are pertinent pieces of information. Things that you feel guilty about and flaws that you perceive in yourself are also very crucial details that you should never share. Divulging these details to a sociopath/psychopath is equivalent to handing one of these people the keys to your emotions. Now, he or she has the power to make you feel afraid, hurt, and happy. Now he or she can manipulate you.

Keep in mind that you may be more resistant to the charms of sociopaths and psychopaths, but other people are not. A good sociopath or psychopath will be able to manipulate other people into sharing information about what makes you tick.

Therefore, you want to be very careful and selective about who you share these details with. It is best to not give this pertinent information to anyone in your life who you do not completely trust. Be prepared for betrayal, sometimes even unwitting and unintentional betrayal from people that you share this information with. It is best to keep this stuff mum from most people.

Don't Share Your Plans

If a sociopath or psychopath knows what your plans are, he or she will try to interfere just to cause mayhem in your life. He or she may also use this knowledge to formulate his or her own nefarious plans. Remember that sociopaths and psychopaths get off on hurting people, and such people will do anything to hurt you. Killing your dreams or plans is a very easy and effective way to hurt you. These harmful people know that, so they will use your plans to their advantage in that endeavor.

It is best to keep your plans to yourself. Don't share your ideas for the future with this type of person ever. Consider your plans to be need-to-know information that you only share with people who need to know them.

What do I mean by plans? Any kind of plan that you have can become corrupted in the hands of a sociopath or psychopath. Don't share your plans for your life, such as moving or working for a promotion at work. Don't share your plans to break up with someone or drop a friend. Especially don't share your dreams and aspirations, as harmful people will trash those plans just to discourage you and hurt you.

Don't Expect a Sociopath to Be Happy for You

Sociopaths despise other people's joy. If you are happy or excited, the sociopathic type or psychopathic type will try to undermine your joy. Therefore, if something good happens to you that excites you or fills you with joy, don't share it with the harmful antisocial type in your life. Keep good news and your happiness to yourself.

If a sociopath or psychopath in your life discovers some sort of joy that you experience, be prepared for negative and hurtful comments aimed at lowering your joy and poisoning your positive attitude with doubt. This is just a game designed to hurt you and make you weak with doubt and negativity. Don't buy into it. When a toxic person belonging to one of the antisocial personality types starts interfering with your happiness, just keep a smile on your face and don't follow his or her line of reasoning. Don't even consider that what he or she says is true. Don't think too much about it. If you do, you are simply second-guessing your capabilities and your aspirations while giving that person the power over you to satisfy his or her selfish desires. Protect your happiness like the precious gift that it is.

Keep Things to Yourself

In fact, it is best to consider keeping things to yourself, a cardinal rule of dealing with these types of people. Don't share or disclose anything that you do not absolutely need to. For instance, if you work with one of these people, you will need to share certain work-related details and pieces of information at times. But you do not have to disclose anything about your personal life or your personal self. Consider this information privileged and do not share it period. This is the perfect ammunition that a sociopath or a Psychopath need to take you out.

Personal information is valuable to sociopaths and psychopaths. They will use what they learn about you to hurt you and manipulate you. The more you share, the more likely the sociopath or psychopath in your life will be able to get hooks into you mentally and emotionally. This is far from a good thing.

Sometimes, other people may not be as wary as you. They may disclose things about you to the harmful person. This harmful person is also probably very adept at fishing for information, so he or she can learn a lot about you without you even oversharing personal information. While you do not want this person to know anything about you, sometimes you just can't help it if he or she finds things out. Do not despair, however. Just because a sociopath or psychopath knows things about you does not mean that you are doomed. Keep your guard up, refuse to share anymore with this person, and don't take his or her attempts to bait you with the information that he or she is privy to.

Confront the Person

Confrontations rarely go well when you are dealing with a twisted sociopathic person. However, they can rid you of this person. Sociopaths and psychopaths like easy targets. If you show that you refuse to be bullied and manipulated, they won't want to waste a lot of time on you. They are more likely to give up and move on to easier victims.

Use confrontation as a means to cut off relationships with these harmful types of people. Don't expect to change them or awaken their inner goodness. No inner goodness exists within them. The confrontation needs to be concise and to the point. Do not do anything in your confrontation except let this person know that you are strong and that you will not tolerate what he or she is putting you through. Don't ask for an apology and don't chastise the person. Just say what you don't like and then move on.

When you confront a sociopath or psychopath, you want to be firm and stand your ground. Do not accuse the person of having a disorder, since you are not a psychologist and cannot reasonably diagnose a person with any sort of mental problem. However, you can address the behavior that you do not care for. Say something like, "I do not care for the drama that you have been causing. You are not going to get what you want from me. It ends now."

You will probably get an argument in response. No sociopath or psychopath will just apologize and admit to wrongdoing. But don't take this bait, for that it is all this is. The person is trying to manipulate you. Instead, just walk away. You have said your piece and there is no need to say anything else. By standing there and arguing, you are setting yourself up for failure and giving this person what he or she wants, which is emotional energy and a mental hook for you. Arguing will not win you anything. So walk away with your head held high and have no more to do with this person.

Don't Be Afraid to Call the Cops

If you fear your safety, don't be afraid to involve the law. Also, do not be afraid to tell people that you have a fear that someone is after you. The more people you have on your side, the more protected you are from this person's psychotic attempts to bully and hurt you.

Unfortunately, if this person has not actually threatened you, there is not much that police can do. But you should collect all evidence of mistreatment and save all text messages or emails that contain threats, no matter how veiled the threats may be. Also, be sure to document any tense or threatening interactions. When you talk to a person who is threatening you, try to always discreetly record the conversation with your phone or some other hidden recording device to capture any threatening behavior. People will probably not believe you until you produce viable proof that this person means to hurt you.

Don't Be Above Professional Help

Sometimes, harmful people are able to undermine your best efforts to protect yourself. Do not feel ashamed. You are dealing with a person who is great at manipulation and who has an iron will. Instead of feeling bad, consider getting some professional counseling to help you learn how to steel yourself against this person and undo any mental or emotional damage that this person has caused you.

Also, counselors are trained to understand and deal with sociopaths and psychopaths. They may be able to give you advice about what you to do. In addition, they are unbiased and will believe you, unlike regular people that you know who may be under the sociopath or psychopath's spell. You can use your counselor as a witness should something bad happen to you because of this dangerous person.

What to Do when You're in a Relationship with a Sociopath or a Psychopath

If you are stuck in an unfortunate relationship with one of these types of people, then you need to get out as soon as possible. You may feel trapped and scared to leave, but you should not remain in this situation longer than you have to. You will start to lose your pride and your identity if you stay with this person too long. This person does not care about you or have your best interests at heart, and he or she will simply use you and leach you dry until you have nothing left to give. Then, he or she will abandon you in a bad situation. You will literally have nothing left and you won't get help from this ex-partner.

Get out now, while you can. Run far, far away. I cannot emphasize this enough. When I stayed in a relationship with a sociopath, I knew that I needed to leave. But I didn't want to, at the same time. I was determined to win this guy's head games and make him love me. I thought that if I fought hard enough, I could earn his affection. He put me through endless pain and I could never win with him until I realized that this relationship was costing me my own identity. I even began thinking and dressing differently, I listened to different music, and I had absolutely no self-esteem or sense of self anymore. Everything was for my man, though he did not do anything for me. He denied me sex, love, and comfort and he loved making me cry. He had even caused me to become isolated from a lot of my family and I had no friends anymore. Finally, I woke up and left. But I wasted six months of my life only to sustain emotional wounds that I still suffer from.

If this person is a family member, just put distance. Seek alternative living arrangements so that you are not under the same roof as this sociopath or psychopath. Also seek healing, which is covered in the next chapter.

If you are romantically involved with this person, really survey your situation. How can you get out? Do you have a safe place to go? Are children involved? Does your partner have financial control over you? Do you feel that he or she may harm your personal safety if you try to bolt? It is best to start setting up a plan to leave. Save some money if you can and find somewhere that you can go, even if it is a shelter. Shelters are not ideal, but they beat remaining at the mercy of some sick and psychotic person who only means you harm. Look into divorce and custody laws in your state or seek free legal help to find out what your options are. You really need to focus on getting your ducks in a row and getting out of your current situation.

If this person is just a friend, you need to step away from the friendship. You will not really be losing anything. You can break things off but it is often easier to just slip away from this person without a confrontation. Stop answering his or her calls and texts. Stop engaging in his or her drama and bait. Remove him or her as a friend on social media.

Finally, if you are dealing with a psychopath or sociopath at work, then you need to leave your job. Ask for a transfer to another branch or find new employment. Otherwise, work on setting boundaries and avoiding this co-worker. Stop sharing personal details with this person or spending time with him or her outside of work. Don't accept any favors from this person, no matter how nice. Don't partake in office drama that this person tries to instigate and don't give this person any information that he or she can create drama with. Stand up to this person and tell him or her off, if you dare.

How to Stop Attracting Sociopaths

Does it seem like you attract sociopathic and psychopathic types? This is not because you are somehow flawed. It is probably because of certain elements of your personality. You can take steps to protect yourself if you seem to be especially vulnerable to these personality types.

Watch Out if You're an Empath

Empaths provide a very special connection that sociopaths and psychopaths can easily exploit. Empaths are caring people who are especially sensitive to the emotional needs of others. Therefore, sociopaths and psychopaths love to put on a show of being emotionally needy, in order to garner the sympathy and commitment of healing empaths. Meanwhile, an empath will strive to please and heal this sociopath or psychopath, giving everything that he or she has to the ill person. He or she will essentially give every bit of oneself until there is nothing left to give.

If you often find yourself becoming the victim of a sociopath or psychopath, then you are probably an empath. Your personality literally acts as a beacon that summons these people. Don't despair yet, however. There are things that you can do to protect yourself from this toxic sociopath-empath connection.

First, you need to determine if you are an empath. A lot of people like to claim that they are empaths when they really are not. A true empath can literally feel the pain and emotions of others. An empath will enter a room and gather vibes from it. Sometimes, the empath will feel sad or happy for no apparent reason; the empath's mood changes are influenced by the moods of others that the empath is around. Finally, an empath has very deep and profound emotional reactions to news and life events. He or she can literally feel when something bad has happened in the world. This large amount of emotional sensitivity can really wear an empath out, so empaths may be introverted and may have discomfort going outside or being in large crowds. This is not because of shyness, but because of the sheer inundation of emotional energy that crowds generate.

Reading that description, do you find that it fits you? If so, then you are probably an empath. This would explain why you attract horrible people. This is not because of some flaw within you. It is because you are a naturally nice and caring person. Because you feel the pain of the world and other people, you are inclined to do something to ease it. You thus like to help people. Sociopaths and psychopaths see your urge to help others as an easily exploitable weakness when really it is a great quality in you. Don't hate yourself for being an empath. Instead, embrace your ability to empathize with others and guard yourself against the harmful people that want to use your natural inclination to help others for their own ends.

For one thing, you want to be more discerning of the people that you let into your life. Don't expend lots of emotional energy on people that you don't know well. You naturally want to help anyone and everyone, which is admirable and sweet. But in this harsh world, consider yourself to be a human swimming in shark-infested waters. You need to get to know people well before you start offering your help to them. Watch out for the signs of sociopathy or psychopathy.

You also need to put your own interests first. Naturally, you want to put others first. This is both admirable and heroic. But more often that not, it will do nothing but hurt you. If someone asks you for a favor that you have to sacrifice your own health or happiness or convenience for, say no. Reserve your energy for yourself and take care of your needs first. When people expect you to put your needs aside for them, politely but blatantly refuse. No good person will ask so much of you.

Finally, take what people say to you with a grain of salt. Listen to your gut. In your haste to help others, you probably often overlook or even flat out ignore your gut. That is why you strive to help sociopaths and psychopaths, even when alarm bells ring in your mind. I knew right away that my ex was off and a little weird, but I ignored that because I valued him as a human being and wanted to help him through his obvious emotional pain. Big mistake. I learned my lesson the hard way and I want to urge you to always listen to your gut. When your gut is saying run away but you start to rationalize your feelings, explain them away, or fall for a sociopath's crocodile tears and superficial charm, you should halt the process. Never try to explain away or ignore your gut. Your first instinct about someone is always right. Words and rationalizations, on the other hand, are usually inaccurate.

When You are Vulnerable

Being in a vulnerable position in life also can leave you bare and ready for the attack of some sociopath or psychopath. Many different circumstances and events can leave you emotionally vulnerable. However, the most common life happenings that make you vulnerable are events where your sense of identity and security becomes threatening. Major life transitions, such as a divorce, tragedies, bouts of physical or mental illness, and tough financial or legal situations such as trials, homelessness, or starvation are all possible causes of emotional vulnerability. You find yourself in a state where you need help and you need a friend. You don't know exactly who you are anymore, or you are unsure of your well-being and safety.

Well, guess who is right there for you? A manipulative, charming person who sees your state of need and is more than happy to help you out. The catch is that this person is a sociopath or psychopath who sees your vulnerability and is ready to take full advantage of you. Whether this person exploits you for sex, emotional brevity, or even money, there will be some ulterior motive to this person's kind and generous actions toward you.

When you find yourself in a bad situation, it is best to not just accept help from the first kind stranger who comes along. Be very cautious and very discerning about the people that you accept help from. Ask people who try to help you what they really want and why they are invested in helping you. Avoid getting into anyone's debt. Try to remain as aloof and independent as you can.

You Don't Love Yourself

Your self-love is so important for your overall well-being. If you don't love yourself, then you don't take care of yourself. You are more willing to accept abysmal treatment from others, such as the treatment that sociopaths and psychopaths will give you. In a way, you are an emotional masochist, who does not mind or even enjoys being emotionally hurt. You feel that you deserve the pain since you believe that you are such a bad person, which is why you enjoy being emotionally used and pummeled by sociopaths.

Your self-loathing may have started in childhood. It may be the result of numerous failures and mistakes that you have made over time in your life. No matter why you believe that you are unworthy of healthy, kind treatment from others and true love, you should not believe these hateful lies about yourself. That is all these self-deprecating thoughts and beliefs are – lies! As a human being, you have intrinsic value. You are not a wholly bad person, even if you have done bad things in the past, and you are redeemable. You have worth, talent, and ability. Your unique personality and appearance alone make you something valuable and beautiful in the world. Do not hate yourself. Find things to love about yourself and only believe in the goodness that you possess.

It is important for you to start treating yourself with some respect. Change how you talk to yourself; talk to yourself like a best friend, instead of criticizing and berating yourself. Don't judge yourself or your flaws so harshly.

Everybody has flaws and you are no different, but there is more good about you than bad. Lead a healthy lifestyle, take care of your body and your health, and make wholesome decisions. Stop engaging in self-destructive habits. When you notice that you accomplish something or when you notice one of your good traits, focus on that rather than your mistakes, failures, and flaws. Choose to see the positive in who you are rather than dwelling on the negative and ruminating on what is wrong in your life. Leave the past behind you and instead focus on building a good present and a bright future. Treat yourself to a spa one day or something pleasurable but healthy every now and then to remind yourself that you are worthy of the best. More than anything, avoid toxic people who talk down to you and hurt your feelings and stand up for your rights as a human being. Surround yourself with better friends.

Even if you don't completely love yourself right now, just changing how you think about yourself and treat yourself can really make a difference. Eventually, you will begin to love yourself more. The more you love yourself, the less abuse you will take. Soon, you will no longer be a magnet for sociopaths or psychopaths, who view your self-loathing as an easy target for their abuse and mind games.

Chapter 6: How to Heal after a Sociopath or Psychopath

Sociopaths and psychopaths do not mind harming you. Not only will they deliberately hurt you just for laughs, but they will also hurt you because they will not hesitate to use you for whatever they can get from you. These sick people will drain you until you have nothing left to give and they will make you feel worthless because they indicate no remorse or regard for your rights. They can use manipulation to batter down your self-esteem, while further proving to you that you do not matter by shamelessly violating your boundaries and your human rights.

When you exit a relationship of any kind with a sociopath or psychopath, you definitely will have some residual of emotional pain. You must take steps to heal yourself and get over the suffering that this person has caused you. Life is too short to suffer forever and you deserve to be happy. Don't allow a sociopath or psychopath to scar you so badly that you never enjoy life ever again.

Acknowledge What Has Happened

Denial and repression will not allow you to heal. Instead, you need to be frank with yourself and acknowledge what you have just been through. Go ahead and think about the horrible things that this person did to you. Let yourself be angry. You can document your feelings in a journal if that helps you process them. You may even find art is a useful expression of what has happened. But just be honest with yourself and others about what you have been through. This helps you start the healing process.

Look on the Bright Side

I firmly believe that everything in life serves a purpose. Finding this purpose can help you get over the negativity of the event that has hurt you. Look on the bright side, try to find the things that you have gained from this experience.

For instance, you have proved to yourself that you are strong, and you have probably learned a lot of good lessons about life and yourself. Now, you have found a purpose for what you have been through. It is probably not so horrible when it doesn't seem totally pointless and useless.

Validate Your Emotions

Every emotion that you feel is legitimate and valid. Your abuser probably told you otherwise, but you have a right to feel the way that you do. Let your emotions flow. Don't repress them or feel guilty about them. Understand that your feelings are uniquely yours and that you are not wrong for feeling them.

Do Not Talk to the Person

Once you get away from a sociopath or psychopath, you need a clean break. If you stay in contact, you only invite more mental control and harm to befall you. Sever all ties and avoid speaking to this harmful person.

Consider Counseling

A professional can help you work through your hurt emotions and damaged thinking. He or she can also teach you how to have healthier relationships in the future. You may enjoy the healing attention that a counselor can give you. You also may benefit from his or her unbiased advice and perspective. A counselor can guide you down a path of attaining self-love and fixing the wounds that made you susceptible to your sociopathic abuser.

Take Some Time for Yourself

You need time to heal. It is not an overnight process. Therefore, don't hop into another relationship right away. If you do, you are inviting another bad person to take advantage of you in your weakened, hurt state. Take some time to yourself to heal. Be patient with yourself. Don't start dating or seeking a new best friend just yet; focus on yourself.

It is OK to be selfish for a while. Your relationship probably called for you to do everything for the sociopath or psychopath. You are literally drained. Finally, you can take some time for yourself and put your needs first. Enjoy this. Take some time to just be selfish, let yourself really heal. Another way in which you could consider helping yourself to heal is, to get involved in programs that offer people like yourself help to recover. This may enlighten and motivate you into realizing that you are not in this alone. The feeling of helping others with their recovery will give you some kind of gratification

Set New Boundaries

As I said earlier, this relationship needs to serve some sort of purpose in your life. Let it be a learning experience. Use it to determine the way that you want to be treated and use it as a way to determine what you do not want in your relationships. With this information, you can create comfortable boundaries that block out harmful people in the future. Always stand behind these boundaries and erect them with every person that you know. Kick people out of your life who do not respect your boundaries.

Don't Feel Sorry for Yourself or be a Victim

It is easy to fall into the trap of feeling sorry for yourself and feeling like a chronic victim. But this only perpetuates the pain that you feel. Instead of pitying yourself, honor how strong you are and what you just survived. Call yourself a survivor, rather than a victim. You are a lot stronger than you realize. Give yourself some credit for once.

Enjoy Yourself

Treat yourself to some joy for once. After suffering for so long, you probably feel like you have been in a black hole. Adding some joy to your life can help free you from this black hole and lift your depression. Do something that you enjoy, even if your abuser told you that this hobby was stupid. Volunteer, take a cool new class and do other activities to make new friends and find the enjoyable side of life again. Be yourself, without paying any mind to the judgments that your abuser cast on you.

Have a Supportive Network

One thing that a sociopath or psychopath may do to you is isolate you. In order to control you, this person has peeled away your social support to make you feel alone and unlovable. That way, he can control your emotions and manipulate you into believing that only he or she could love you so that you would not leave. Once you leave this relationship, you should seek the comfort and love of your friends and family again. They will probably still love you, and they will be relieved to know that you are finally free of the horrible person that you were with. Their love will help you feel better. You will realize that you do have worth as a person and that you are lovable.

Conclusion

Sociopaths are sick, harmful people who have become ill mainly thanks to their upbringing. Psychopaths are calculating, reptilian people who cannot feel proper human emotions and do not care for the well-being of others. Their disorder arises from their abnormal brain structures, which can be caused by birth injury or genetics. Both types of people belong to a special psychological group called Antisocial Personality Disorder. Indeed, both are undoubtedly antisocial, as they do not have normal social skills or any desire to care for other people.

If you ever wonder what goes on in a sociopath's or psychopath's mind, then look no further than this book. The stories and profiles contained in Chapters 3 and 4 offer rich insight into the viewpoints and emotions of these antisocial people. It is important to understand how these people think and process emotion since together, they comprise of at least two percent of the human population. It is very likely that you have encountered at least one of these people in your lifetime.

If you have encountered one of these people, then I am deeply sorry. The emotional wreckage that these selfish and unemotional people leave behind them in every relationship is unparalleled. If you have known a sociopath or psychopath, then you probably now suffer from some sort of emotional wound or damage. This is because sociopaths and psychopaths manipulate and hurt others remorselessly just to get what they want. You were used as a pawn, and now you have seen the worst of human nature. It can be hard to get over the exposure to a true sociopath or psychopath. The damage may be even worse if you had prolonged exposure to one, such as you dated one or were raised by one.

Fortunately, you have now read this book. You have gained a better understanding of these people, so you know how to protect yourself in the future. You also understand that what happened to you was in no way your fault. You were an innocent victim of a sick, conniving person who was incapable of caring about you. The fault lies on the person who hurt you; it does not lie on you.

You should never feel stupid for falling for a sociopath or psychopath's tricks since these types of people are naturally very charming and enigmatic. You did not know that this person was as harmful as he or she turned out to be. We would all have a perfect life if we had the ability to predict the future and know the intentions of others. Yes, you were cleverly fooled. This is also not your fault. At least now you know what to watch out for.

Healing from sociopathic or psychopathic abuse can be a long and slow process. But once you heal, you will find that you are stronger than ever before. While the sociopath or psychopath who hurt you did not care if you lived or died, you did live. Now you are more adept at protecting yourself and you are better able to guard yourself against future harm. You have learned and grown strong. Adopt a thankful attitude for the good that came from your horrible experience, look on the bright side, and move on. Arm yourself with the knowledge that you survived the worst imaginable and that you deserve much better treatment.

In the future, you should avoid these harmful and toxic people. But don't let the wounds that they inflicted on you hold you back from love and success. You can have great lovers and friends who are not out to manipulate you, use you, and hurt you for the joy of it. Instead, there are many good people out there. You may feel afraid to love again or to get close to anyone, but don't be. Just watch out for the signs of psychopathy and sociopathy that I listed in an earlier chapter. Guard yourself. Make sure that you know people very well and know their histories before you let them into your life and your heart.

Chances are, you will not encounter too many sociopaths or psychopaths in your lifetime. The number of these people is relatively small compared to population size. However, if you feel like you attract these types of people, you may be an easy victim. Take better care of yourself by watching out for charming people. Don't make yourself easy to manipulate. If something does not feel right in your gut, then trust yourself and run the other way. This book can help you steel yourself against these harmful people so that you can stop getting hurt.

Remember that you attract what you think that you are worth, so if you feel unworthy of love or care, then you are more likely to invite people like sociopaths and psychopaths into your life. By loving yourself first and above all, you can avoid having such people in your life. People will respect you more and you will feel better about yourself and who you are as a person.

This book can really help you improve the quality of your life. Using the advice contained in these pages, you can effectively spot and avoid psychopaths and sociopaths, since you understand their traits and what they act like. You can also heal yourself from the emotional damage that these people inflicted upon you. Start loving yourself more and ridding your life of sick, toxic people who offer you no personal benefit. Everything will be OK. You will come out ahead. Enjoy your life and kick out the people who make it less enjoyable. Care for yourself and don't let sick people tend to your emotional needs, as they will always take advantage of you and hurt you. With 'The True Intentions of Sociopaths and Psychopaths Revealed' in these pages, you can now understand why It is really that SIMPLE!

Thank you for reading!

Sources

Griffith, S. (2015). *How to Spot a Psychopath*. Daily Mail. Retrieved from http://www.dailymail.co.uk/sciencetech/article-3379996/How-spot-psychopath-Expert-reveals-traits-look-charm-eccentricity-manipulation.html.

Ohikuare, J. (2014). *Life as a Nonviolent Psychopath*. The Atlantic. Retrieved from http://www.theatlantic.com/health/archive/2014/01/life-as-a-nonviolent-psychopath/282271/.

Parry, W. (2011). *How to Spot Psychopaths: Their Speech Patterns Give Them Away*. LiveScience. Retrieved from http://www.livescience.com/16585-psychopaths-speech-language.html.

Thomas, M. E. (2014). *Confessions of a Sociopath: A Life Spent Hiding in Plain Sight*. Broadway Books: Portland, OR. ISBN: 978-0307956651.

Quora.

Was My Ex a Sociopath? (2013). Experience Project. Retrieved from http://www.experienceproject.com/stories/Am-A-Sociopath/3340264.